ROBERT READING TO HIS FATHER. Page 34.

Clean Your Boots, Sir?

THE

History of Robert Rightheart.

A STORY FOR BOYS.

2 Samuel, xxii.29

Lamplighter Publishing.

Waverly, Pennsylvania.

United States of America.

Prologue.

During this past year disturbing events have knocked at the door of the weak conscience of our nation. Children are killing children.

Though these acts of senseless killing are unthinkable, they are not new. Six thousand years ago, the very first act of murder was recorded when Cain killed his brother Abel. Approximately forty-five hundred years ago, the Bible states that the whole earth was filled with violence. Two thousand years ago, there was also unrest within a nation. Babies were slaughtered (as they are today) and a nation lived without hope. But there was One who extended unconditional forgiveness and acceptance that turned despair into hope and violence into love.

Today our children are growing in a society where acceptance often seems to be found among peers or gang members, resulting in deviant behavior. The solution for our current crisis is not found in gun control, safer schools, more counselors, or more government intervention. No, the solution is found in a God who loves us and gave Himself for us. It is found in the God of "out-stretched arms". The solution is also found in God's people: "If my people, who are called by my name, shall humble themselves and pray, and seek my face, and turn from their wicked ways, then will I hear from heaven, and will forgive their sin, and will heal their land."

Our children need to see the Living God *living* in us. They need to see His people living justly, loving mercy and walking humbly with our God. They need to see us living not by our own strength and selfish pursuits, but in lowliness of mind, esteeming others better than ourselves.

Our children need to see our walk speaking louder than our words. In this little story you are about to read, you will be challenged by a walk that speaks louder than words. May many children be inspired to follow the noble example of Robert Rightheart and be brave enough to stand for what is right!

To the King of Righteousness,

Mark Hamby

Dedication.

I would like to first thank our gracious Lord for allowing our ministry the privilege of publishing literature that can be used to change lives for eternity. May You continue to do exceedingly abundantly above all that we could ask or think, and may we maintain the integrity and faithfulness that allows your blessing to continue. Thank you, Stacey Devon, for entrusting this treasure with Lamplighter Publishing. I know that God will use this work to turn the hearts of fathers and sons to make ready a people prepared for the Lord.

I would like to thank my wife Debbie for the hours of unselfish proofreading, sketching and designing. You are truly a faithful wife. Debbie Nichols, thank you so much for your servant's heart to help us when we needed help - especially when time was running out. Shannon Johnson, you have been a breath of fresh air since you came on staff. Your work and faithfulness are a blessing and a reflection of the truths found in this little book.

The decision to print *Clean Your Boots, Sir?* did not take long. It was read in one sitting and immediately I knew that honor, integrity, sacrifice, love, faithfulness, and character of the highest level were portrayed for boys in the same inspiring manner that Mary demonstrated these values in *The Basket of Flowers*. I believe that it was you, Stacey, who said, "I have found a book equal to *The Basket of Flowers*, only for boys!" Yes, indeed you have.

In hope of His soon return,

Mark Hamby

2 Chronicles, xvi. 9a.

CLEAN YOUR BOOTS, SIR?

Copyright © 1999 by Mark A. Hamby
Selected Illustrations: Copyright ©1999,
Lamplighter Publishing.
First Printing, April, 1999

Published by Lamplighter Publishing; A division of
Cornerstone Family Ministries, Inc.
P. O. Box 777, Waverly, PA 18471

The Lamplighter Rare Collector's Series is a series
of family Christian literature from the 17th, 18th, &
19th centuries. Each edition is printed in an
attractive hard-bound collector's format. For more
information, write: Lamplighter Publications, P.O.
Box 777, Waverly, PA 18471 or call (570) 585-1314.

Author: Anonymous
Illustrations and artists: Unknown
Cover Design: Deborah J. Hamby
Printed in the United States of America
ISBN 1-58474-015-9

CONTENTS.

CHAPTER I.
BOB AT HIS BOOT-BLOCK 9

CHAPTER II.
DARK DAYS 23

CHAPTER III.
BOB FINDS NEW FRIENDS 41

CHAPTER IV.
BOB SAILS FOR CALCUTTA 49

CHAPTER V.
A STRANGE OCCURRENCE 65

CHAPTER VI.
THE TRIAL 73

CHAPTER VII.
THE RETURN TO ENGLAND 81

CHAPTER VIII.
MARY MILCOMBE AND THE MARRIAGE DAY 91

CHAPTER IX.
ROBERT'S HOME IN CALCUTTA 103

CLEAN YOUR BOOTS, SIR?

CHAPTER I.

BOB AT HIS BOOT-BLOCK.

"LET me whisper a secret to you," said Annie Fielding, with a roguish smile upon her face, to her little brother Martin. "There are no lessons this morning; we're going to the City with Papa."

"Hurrah!" said Martin, who was putting a new sail into his boat in the arbor at the end of the garden. "I'm precious glad of it; I want to buy a brass anchor, and there's a shop in Cornhill where they keep beauties. I mean to fix it here, you know," he said, pointing to the prow of his tiny ship; "then it will be like a real East Indiaman."

"Make haste, then," said Annie, adding the emphasis of a shake to her brother's shoulder. "Come on, Marty dear; finish the sail when you come back."

In a short time, one on each side of their father, they went speeding along full of the pleasant anticipations of a childish holiday. The omnibus soon came in sight, and after taking up a passenger here and there along the Terrace, when it reached our little friends, to Martin's great delight there was only room for one inside, so he had the pleasure of a mount up outside with his father.

It was Christmas-time, and a very sharp Christmas-time indeed. The frost had been much more severe than had been known for many a year. That morning the frost was beginning to break up. The Strand, along which they passed, was a scene of great confusion; first one omnibus horse and then another fell with a heavy thud on the slippery road, and helped to block up the already crowded thoroughfare; cabs,

CLEAN YOUR BOOTS, SIR?

carts, and vans seemed to be inextricably jumbled together, and there was quite an exciting amount of shouting and commotion.

The City was, however, reached at last, and the three had now to make a run for it across to the Royal Exchange. It is a difficult crossing at the best, and they landed, with an "Oh, dear me" from Annie, who was out of breath, close to the statue which stands in front of the Exchange, - the chief use of which seems to be to keep the wind and sleet in winter, and the hot sun in summer, off the red-coated lads who clean boots beneath its shadow.

What a merry-looking lot they are, these busy shoeblack boys; and what varieties of character comes to them. Who knows what great men's faces they look up to, sometimes, in their honest toil? It is quite amusing to think what strange diversities of customers they get; sometimes costermongers, sometimes clergymen, sometimes scavengers, sometimes statesmen, sometimes fast men, sometimes farmers. Yes; all come to the red-coated owners of the black-boxes to have their boots brightened by the boys.

Mr. Fielding stopped a moment or two to watch the busy scene, and to remind Martin that honest industry is always beautiful, even if the occupation was that of cleaning boots. "Remember, my boy," he said, "that it is not so much *who* we are, as *what* we are, that entitles us to honor and respect."

Presently, one of the boot-blacks was disengaged, and a little lad in his red regiment was waiting for a customer; he had a quick, intelligent face - who was he? We must devote a few pages to some sketch of his history.

His name was Robert Rightheart, and a real good fellow he is. If you watch him, as he kneels before his black-box in the morning, you will see what a cheery sort of way he has with him; he settles himself down, plays a tune on the top of his box with the back of his brushes, takes the alto in the shape of a whistle, and winds up

CLEAN YOUR BOOTS, SIR?

with the familiar sentence, "Clean your boots, sir?"

This morning, however, he had come to work rather depressed and dull; he had omitted his usual musical entertainment; with a heavy heart he had left his home, and the walk evidently had not worked off his trouble. Robert lived in a little house in Prospect Place, which, like most places so named, is up a dark and dingy court with a blank wall in front, and a row of black chimney pots at the back. He left an aged father at home, who is the victim of paralysis, and two little brothers; they are younger than Robert, and are motherless, for in the cholera season the mother died suddenly, and the severe shock brought paralysis on the father; they have little as a family to support them, they get a trifle from the parish, the elder of the two little ones holds horses, runs errands, carries parcels, and sometimes earns fourpence a day. Robert earns all else that they get.

Now Robert has watched his father very closely lately, and a tear has often silently stolen down the lad's cheek, as he sees how much that father needs a strengthening diet; how he keeps sinking, his life ebbing away like the outgoing tide. Robert sees too, how badly the little brothers need new shoes. Poor boy! He can clean them but he cannot make them; he has also an idea that he will try and buy an extra blanket for father this cold, cold winter-time. Sometimes Robert saves; then comes a bad day or two, and his little bank, like many a big one, begins to break. Last evening, for instance, he was obliged to dip rather deeply into his little store to supply home necessities; for on wet days and foggy days gentlemen cannot keep their boots bright, and so don't come to have them cleaned at all.

Thus it happened that to-day, being rather heavy-hearted, Robert was tuneless when he spread his little odd bit of carpet and knelt down before his box. His first customer was a youth with dishevelled hair and dirty collar, who had a very dissipated look indeed, as if he had been up all night, and had his breakfast at a coffee-stall after disgracing himself at a casino; he hummed a merry tune, but Robert thought he looked very miserable after all, for his face seemed to say that such "mirth was madness." Robert knew his Bible well; he had been taught in a ragged school close by the little court where his mother died, and he had early learned to love and serve the Saviour; his teacher had been made a greater blessing to him than any words can tell; he was in darkness, she showed him the light; he was a poor, lost boy, she showed him the way of pardon and peace through a crucified Redeemer! Not only, however, by *what* she taught, but by her own peculiar personal influence, did his dear teacher win his heart for Christ. She was a Christian lady of gentle manners and graceful mien, with love to the world's lost ones in her heart; and she had gained, first the attention of Robert Rightheart to herself, and then was successful in leading him to the Lamb of God who taketh away the sin of the world. Robert often pondered the question what might have become of him if he had never entered the

Ragged School, especially if he had never had such a forebearing, kind teacher; his poor mother had been kind to him, very kind, but she could not teach him that of which she knew so little; this Christian lady had been a mother to him in the best sense, and he never rose or rested, without thanking God for such a friend, and praying that to many more little lost London Arabs like himself, she might be the means of rescue from sin. Remembering, then, this incident in Robert's history, you need not be surprised that he looked upon the fast, and gaily dressed youth, whose boots he had just made shine so brightly, with pity rather than with envy.

His next customer was a city clerk, who had made an awkward slip that morning in getting off a Chelsea omnibus, and needed freshening up a bit. Robert looked at him as he trudged off to Prince's Street, and wondered whether the day would ever come when *he* should rise to be a city clerk, and have some little lad to clean *his* boots for him; his spirits were beginning to

CLEAN YOUR BOOTS, SIR?

get a little better now, for the coppers were coming in briskly, and he warmed to his work both in mind and body.

It was just at this moment that Mr. Fielding, Martin, and Annie, were watching Robert's face as he looked up and down and all around, wistfully watching for some new customer to his block. Presently a burly sort of farmer made his way straight for the vacant boot-box; he had a broad, honest countenance, and having just come from the corn market in Mark Lane, was on his way to the Great Eastern Railway, to get home by the train. See, here he comes across the road; take care! you omnibus; *he's coming*, and it's better not to run the chance of his upsetting you! It was no light work cleaning *his* boots, and the big drops of perspiration glistened upon Robert's brow; first, there was the half-frozen conglomeration of the farm-yard which he got at five o'clock in the morning when he went round the sheds to see the young heifers attended to; then there was the thick clay down the New Road to

CLEAN YOUR BOOTS, SIR?

Mudmarsh Station; and as an overall, there was the black London sludgy grease. Now the farmer, though a very honest man, was not fond of over-payments; so after all Bob's hot hard work, he put his hand into his capacious pocket, made all the money chink, and then handed Bob two halfpence. Robert took them in his fingers, then touched his cap with them, and away went the burly farmer.

Mr. Fielding had been busy telling his little charge about the Mansion House, and the Bank, and the fearful fire which raged so close to where they stood, when the old Exchange was burned down; he was now about to lead them on to the anchor shop in Cornhill, when he heard one of the shoeblack boys exclaim, "All that for a penny, Bob?" - for they had seen the farmer give Robert the two halfpence, while one of them had just got a silver threepenny for polishing a fast man's boots that were only slightly soiled.

"Never mind," said Bob. "Better luck next time!" He was about to drop the coppers into the black box and enjoy the

CLEAN YOUR BOOTS, SIR?

merry chink, when lo! Something gleamed from between the halfpence. It was a shilling! No! It was a sovereign!!!

At once Bob saw all his morning's dream realized; the blankets, and the boots, and the port wine for father; at once his heart leapt up, his tongue was unloosed, while the surrounding lads flourished their brushes and gave a hearty too-ril-lil-a on the back of their boxes for very joy!

"Halves!" cried the boy next to him; but Robert tuned pale - his hope was dying out - the blanket prospect was fast fading away like a dissolving view. Would it be right to keep it? This was the consideration just now rather puzzling to his thought. Then the devil entered into the poor boy's heart and plied his cleverest weapons of war; he at once suggested many excuses to him for keeping the sovereign to himself; such as these: that he didn't know where the farmer was going; that he needed it far more than the hearty farmer did; that he would be little likely to overtake him after so many minutes had elapsed.

CLEAN YOUR BOOTS, SIR?

But the devil got the worst of it. Robert had learned the sweet lesson of going to the Strong for strength. He knew full well that he could lift up his little heart to God in the street or by the wayside, as well as in the closet, and with a speechless earnestness he sought the Lord, and the Lord heard him. Down went his brushes. "Mind my box, he said; he saw the track the farmer took, and gathering up his apron, away he sped at a pace which aroused the curiosity of many passers by.

Mr. Fielding stood like one transfixed; he had been standing unperceived pretty close to Bob, just under the side shadow of the Statue, and had heard all that passed. The whole scene had so arrested his thought that for the time being, this little heroism of humble life filled him with a fascination and a wonder which he could scarcely conceal.

"Brave boy!" he said to himself; "what a plucky little chap he is! I wonder what memorable scene in history has more of the real heroic in it than this? I wonder if there are many such unknown heroes

CLEAN YOUR BOOTS, SIR?

amongst the poor and forgotten." As he thus mused, his feeling of interest took such hold on him that he resolved to await Bob's return to the box; so taking the little folks into a neighboring pastry cook's, he left them for awhile, and placed himself in a position of observation as undemonstratively as he could.

Meanwhile we must follow Robert as he pressed on his way. Like a hound upon the scent he sped along the streets. Some dandies, I can assure you, got finely splashed that day. Away! away! now on the path, now off; past the Exchange, up Threadneedle Street, into Bishopgate Street; then the course was clearer. He guessed that the farmer would be making for the station. On Robert ran quite out of breath; - but ah! there's the farmer! no, that's not his face, but he has the same broad build; they are all so much alike, these Essex farmers. Off again went Bob, up to the very gateway to the Station. Yes; there he is, that's the gentleman. One more bound - on and off the pavement again, now he has seized his heavy coat-tails.

"P-please sir, you left a p-o-und between the halfpennies."

"Aye? What? Hullo! Ah!" says the farmer; and dived his hand into the depth of his breeches pocket and counted his cash. Truth to tell, there was a very careless conglomeration of sovereigns, sixpences, and half-pennies, in the said pocket, for which habit of promiscuous muddling together of money his good lady at home had scolded him often enough.

"Yes, my lad, I'm a pound short, clear enough. Thankee, my boy, thankee," said the farmer; here's a FIVE-SHILLING PIECE FOR YOU."

Five shillings! Ah! that was indeed well-earned money, that was. It would have been scarcely right for the farmer to reward virtue with all, and so give Bob the sovereign; but he did very right to give him a good round sum, and leave him still the sweet satisfaction of having made a sacrifice for the truth.

CHAPTER II.

DARK DAYS.

ROBERT soon hastened back to his boot-box. If you could have caught just a glimpse of his radiant countenance, all aglow with heat and with excitement, you would have seen in his eye a gleam of light which bespoke the gladness of his heart: for Robert was happy, very happy; he had conquered the suggestions of the great enemy of souls, and in the little sphere of his being there was fulfilled the words, "then the devil left him, the angels came and ministered unto him." What a sweet musical peal there rang in the belfry of poor Robert's heart. All the clear chimes of conscience pealed out the pleasant couplet—"Well done, Rightheart! Well done, Bob!"

CLEAN YOUR BOOTS, SIR?

His face had not lost its flush, nor his eye its lustre when he got back again to the boot-boxes and the boys. Although he had been rapid enough in his pursuit of the farmer, and in his return had scarcely rested save to buy a penny orange of a poor woman with a child in her arms, whom he often saw and pitied as she toiled home his way at night,--still it was some time before he returned, and Mr. Fielding was almost tired of waiting; but he was not sorry in the end that he had patiently delayed.

"What a soft!" said one of the shoe-blacks, "to give the old 'un back his money." "A regular fool," said another. But Bob knew he was no fool. Fools never had such sweet satisfaction in a sense of duty nobly done as he felt then. Bob held up aloft his bright crown-piece with a look of triumph, and said, "Look there, my lads! What d'ye think of that?"

Mr. Fielding seized his opportunity, and stepped up to the block to have his boots cleaned. "What's your name, my boy?" he asked.

CLEAN YOUR BOOTS, SIR?

Robert looked up with his glistening hazel eye, and said, "Robert Rightheart, sir."

"And where do you live?"

"In Prospect Place."

"Can you write it down for me?"

"Yes, sir; all right," said Robert, wondering whatever purpose the gentleman could have in view; but there was a kindliness in his voice and manner, which touched him in his then frame of mind very deeply.

"Here's my pocket-book, then," said Mr. Fielding; "jot it down yourself."

Robert put the book on the black-box and forthwith, in a clear, steady hand, wrote upon a blank sheet his name and address. Perhaps the writing was a little in schoolboy fashion; but for all that, the letters were well shaped, and it was clearly and carefully done.

Mr. Fielding bade him good day, and then hurried off to Martin and Annie, who were glad enough to escape from the pastry-cook's parlor, and get off to doll shops and boat shops, and other pleasant places. Gleefully enough therefore they hastened along the already crowded streets. Oh what happy, happy days these childhood ones are; wise indeed are those parents who temper authority with kindness; who are as careful to provide pleasures, as they are lessons, for the young. A pleasant childhood is a sweet landscape in the distance, to which the heart of man ever looks back with gratitude and joy, amid all the trials, duties, and temptations of life.

We must now leave this happy trio to pursue their pleasant way. The father, glad in the children's joy, and refreshed by the manifest zest which they felt in life; and they, forgetful of all else but the purchases they wanted to make, and the pleasant excitement of the day.

But Robert requires our attention, and to his history we must now return. He had a wonderfully good day at his boot-block; it turned out to be a profitable one in every sense; he had lots of customers, and as some of them had their boots very dirty indeed, they considerately tossed him a silver three-penny. About half-past six o'clock, Bob shut up shop; that is to say, he put the bung carefully into his blacking-pot, put his brushes inside the box, rolled up his kneeling carpet, and then, as a finale, and with the hand of a master in the art, swung the whole establishment over his shoulder, and trudged off home, whistling a cheery tune as he wended his accustomed way to Prospect Place.

Just as he turned the corner of the street in the centre of which this same Prospect Place was situated, he met his little brother Jim, and ran full tilt against him. "Hullo, little man!" Robert said; "What on earth's the matter? What's the matter, eh?" he said more urgently, as he looked at the little fellow's downcast face.

"Father's so bad;" sobbed Jim," so very bad, and I'm going for Mr. Minton."

Now Mr. Minton was the parish doctor, a kind-hearted, attentive man; and for the honor of his name be it spoken, as attentive to the humblest patients as though they belonged to the wealthy or the noble.

"I do hope he'll come," said little Jim, with big tears in his eye; "Father's very bad."

"What is it?" said Robert.

"Father's ill; a kind of second fit, like," said Jim; "and he hardly moves or breathes."

Robert waited to hear no more. This conversation occupied but a hasty minute, and he rushed on up the court, having told him to run as fast as his legs could carry him to the doctor's house.

When he got up-stairs into the little room with the sloping roof, he saw at one glance that his father was very ill, with a deadly ashiness on his lips; he was lying on the bed with his head hanging downward towards the floor. Robert tenderly lifted his head on to the pillow, wetted his lips with water, and seeing that consciousness was coming back, he whispered, "You're very ill, Father."

The voice made a faint effort to reply, but failed; at length he said, "Yes, but it's all right, Bob, my boy;--all right."

CLEAN YOUR BOOTS, SIR?

Robert almost wondered what he meant, but he inclined in that moment to the happy thought that his taciturn father knew more about the Saviour than he had previously thought; for being one of those very reserved people who do not like to tell their thoughts, it was not easy to draw his ideas from him on any subject, especially on religion. Robert felt, however, that this was the time, indeed, to satisfy himself that all was well with him.

"I feel a little better now, Bob," the father said; " but WHERE'S HE?"

"Where's who?" said Robert. "Jim's gone for the doctor; and Mr. Minton will be here, depend upon it, very soon; his kind heart will not keep him from any poor man that's very ill."

"Nay, Bob, I didn't mean the lad or the doctor," said the sick patient. "I suppose I fainted like, just now; but I've felt like dying all day long, and a hymn as you sing about heaven with the little ones on Sunday afternoons came into my mind."

"I know," said Bob, and he repeated the hymn:

"Beautiful Zion, built above,
  Beautiful city that I love,
  Beautiful gates of pearly white,
  Beautiful temple, God its light.

  Beautiful heaven where all is light,
  Beautiful angels clothed in white,
  Beautiful strains that never tire,
  Beautiful harps through all the choir.

  Beautiful crowns on every brow,
  Beautiful palms the conquerors show,
  Beautiful robes the ransomed wear,
  Beautiful all who enter there.

  Beautiful throne of Christ our King,
  Beautiful songs the angels sing,
  Beautiful rest, all wanderings cease,
  Beautiful home of perfect peace."

"Yes," said the father, and his lips muttered, "Beautiful! But think of that other, Bob; you know, about Him."

Robert's hopes were all alive now; that repeated utterance, HIM, made him

CLEAN YOUR BOOTS, SIR?

conscious that it was indeed the Christ of whom his father was then thinking, and on whom he trusted indeed that he was leaning. He had not difficulty in recalling the sweet hymn of Newton's:

"One there is above all others,
  Well deserves the name of Friend;
His is love beyond a brother's,
  Costly, free, and knows no end;
They who once His kindness prove,
Find it everlasting love.

Which of all our friends to save us,
  Could or would have shed his blood?
But the Saviour died to have us
  Reconciled in Him to God;
This was boundless love indeed!
Jesus is a Friend in need.

O for grace our hearts to soften;
  Teach us, Lord, at length to love;
We, alas! forget too often,
  What a Friend we have above;
But when home our souls are brought,
We shall love Thee as we ought."

"Yes," said the dying man, "that's the ONE; I thought about HIM; and then He came and whispered to me; leastways I thought so."

Robert was a manly little fellow, and did not hesitate to ask a question near to his heart; and he said, rather nervously, but boldly, " and you've committed all to HIM, Father?"

"Yes, boy; yes, boy."

"And do you love HIM, Father?"

"Well, I didn't use to, Bob; mind ye, though, I didn't know much about Him. But then, it's different lately. I've been very dull and lone since your mother died; and of a Sunday afternoon, when you and the little ones have been singing, I've learnt a bit like here and there; and lately, when you have been out a city missionary's kindly come in, and he's talked to me about sin and the Saviour; he's prayed with me wonderful too, as though he knowed all as was in me. At last I felt very different - quite changed like; and it did melt my poor heart to think as the Lord Jesus died for me."

CLEAN YOUR BOOTS, SIR?

ROBERT READING TO HIS FATHER. Page 34.

CLEAN YOUR BOOTS, SIR?

Poor man! saying all this in his broken way had made him tired and faint. After a little he beckoned to Bob, and said, "Read a bit, and pray with me, Bob!"

The poor lad's voice was very husky, but he read some verses from the Bible, and then offered a very earnest prayer. There was a dew of tears upon both faces, when the simple service was over; but the lines of pain seemed to have melted out of his father's face, and a holy peace reigned alike in both their hearts. It was sad indeed to have to lose that father; but who can tell the gladness of his boy's heart, to know that for him to die would be gain.

A brisk footstep was soon heard on the creaking old stairs, and in came the kind and active Mr. Minton. Parish doctors are not the flinty-hearted men they are sometimes described as being, but are for the most part attentive and careful even to the poorest; their pay is very small, and their labor very great.

"Well, what's amiss?" said the doctor, as he took the hand of the patient in his own.

CLEAN YOUR BOOTS, SIR?

"Ah, there's mischief here," said he, as he felt the weak and fluttering pulse; "he mustn't talk much, and he must have nourishing food."

Robert spoke up at once. "I can get it for him, sir. Anything you order, sir. What shall it be, sir?"

Mr. Minton looked round with a significant smile. "Are you a nabob?" he said.

"I don't know what that is, sir," said Robert respectfully; "but I've got ten shillings and more."

"Well," said the doctor, "you'll want it all, my good boy; but go and get a nice piece of beef, and I will tell you how to make some good beef-tea."

Robert found Mr. Minton in this and every after-visit a friend indeed.

Day after day came and went, with that lingering heaviness which time assumes when there is sickness at home. The doctor called night and morning. Little Jim was left at home as head nurse, while Robert went to his post in front of the Exchange.

CLEAN YOUR BOOTS, SIR?

Ah, as we ride on an omnibus, or even have our boots cleaned, we little know what heavy hearts may be close to us, and how often they pass us in the street. If we did know, we should be more considerate than we are; some are thinking of a lost competency,-some of a dying father,-some of a sick wife or child. But Robert found a world of comfort these sad days in lifting up his heart from the cold pavement to the skies, and casting all his boyhood's care on Christ.

It was not long before the end came; his father was gradually nearing the great haven of rest, and on Saturday evening he opened his eyes on Robert, and said, "God bless you, Bob!"

Bob sat down beside him, and tried to comfort him. "You've been a kind boy to me, Bob," he said, "and there's One as'll take care of you when I'm gone. Say another hymn to me, Bob."

It was an interesting spectacle. Jim and his wee brother Dickie sat on their little wooden stools, and Bob sat beside the bed. The moon was just rising, and peeping in

CLEAN YOUR BOOTS, SIR?

through the casement. Taking his father's hand in his own, Bob repeated softly and slowly the words:

"Though often here we're weary,
　There is sweet rest above,
A rest that is eternal,
　Where all is peace and love;
Oh let us then press forward
　That glorious rest to gain;
We'll soon be free from sorrow,
　From toil and care and pain.
　　There is a sweet rest in heaven.

"Our Saviour will be with us
　E'en to our journey's end;
In every sore affliction,
　His present help to lend;
He never will grow weary,
　Though often we request;
He'll give us grace to conquer,
　And take us home to rest.
　　There is a sweet rest in heaven."

Gently pressing his father's hand, he felt a slight tremor in it, and while Bob uttered the words, the father's spirit knew their fuller meaning, for he had "entered into rest."

Mr. Minton came in and found his poor patient gone. The city missionary also called, and kindly comforted the little lads. The parish buried him. Poor Bob wasn't rich enough for that. It was with a brave courage, however, that he followed his father to the grave, with a little brother in each hand, and the beautiful words fell like dew upon his heart - "I am the resurrection and the life, said the Lord."

It was harder work still to bear the solitude of the little room which so reminded him of the dead; but he did that. He still rented the apartment in Prospect Place. He rose a little earlier, and went to bed a little later; and with the aid and sympathy of a Christian lady who visited the court as part of her Bible district, he got on pretty well. She kindly sent some bundles of clothes for the little brothers, and on the whole Bob was prosperous enough. On Sunday afternoon you might see the three trudging along to the ragged school together - Bob as a teacher, and Jim and Dickie as scholars. Robert resolved never to forget God, and God in great mercy remembered him.

CHAPTER III.

BOB FINDS NEW FRIENDS.

IT is necessary now to turn our attention for a time to Mr. Fielding, and the enthusiastic young couple with him. The brass anchor had been obtained, and Annie had purchased a splendid doll that opened and shut its eyes, and which, when set upon its feet was half her own height - such a doll as seems in every generation to be a most coveted possession. After making a few other purchases, and visiting the Tower, they were returning through Cornhill, when Mr. Fielding met a very old and dear friend, an officer belonging to the East India Company, who, after some years of hard service, had just returned to his native land. Captain Summer was a hearty, genial-spirited man, though somewhat weakened by a long residence in the East, where he had earned the respect and love of his friends, as well as a handsome pension from the Government; he hoped, now that he was about to enjoy retirement and rest, to meet from time to time at his club and at his residence, those dear friends who had served with him abroad, and whom he had now returned to mingle amongst at home. It needed very little pressing to induce him to spend the evening at Mr. Fielding's house.

They were soon engaged in that after-dinner chat which is so eagerly entered upon by friends who have been long separated by land and wave. In the course of the evening, when conversation had flagged a little, Mr. Fielding related with great zest and animation his little adventure in connection with Robert Rightheart; and the Captain, who could appreciate the heroic in humble life, as well as in the field of war, cried out "Capital! Capital! What a hidden hero you have hit upon, old friend!"

CLEAN YOUR BOOTS, SIR?

"This is the place of his hiding then," said Mr. Fielding, drawing out his pocketbook - "That's the direction - and he wrote it himself!"

"He's worth somebody's looking after, that lad is; there's little doubt of that," said the Captain. The conversation turned now to other matters, and for a time poor Bob and his heroism were quite forgotten.

Two or three months afterwards, as the Captain and Mr. Fielding were coming arm in arm from the Gresham club, where they had been dining together with a friend, who should they spy passing the end of King William Street but Bob, returning home after his hard day's work.

Forthwith they resolved to follow him, and a long queer sort of march they had of it. They passed onwards to Shoreditch, with its densely crowded back neighborhood, and after crossing three or four very dingy streets they arrived at last at Prospect Place.

Bob, little knowing what detectives were that day dogging his steps, hummed a tune or two as he hastened on his way. He heard steps behind him, however, blundering up the dark staircase, and looking down saw two figures; and as they stepped into his room, with an apology for surprising him, Robert recognized in the features of one of them, the gentleman who had his boots cleaned on the memorable five-shilling day, and to whom he had given his address.

"Please to sit down, gentlemen," said Robert.

Captain Summers, in his familiar style, called out at once, "So we will, my lad;" and addressing Mr. Fielding, said, "Let's come to an anchor, old friend, at once."

Now the room was very clean and very tidy. The poor do help the poor! All had been got ready for Bob by an old woman lodging in the house, who did what she could for the orphan family without fee or reward. All that Robert could do for her was to polish her old man's boots before he went out to his own daily toil. It was a sort of "quid pro quo," but it wasn't much.

The room was clean, and that was a good deal to say for such a poor, shaky sort of

CLEAN YOUR BOOTS, SIR?

tenement, and so were the two little lads, who looked startled enough to see the strangers come in.

"Are you afraid of losing these youngsters?" said the Captain, addressing Bob.

Robert turned pale. They looked well enough, he thought, certainly they weren't ill.

"Losing them, did you say, sir?" said he, his bright hazel eye glistening with a tear. "I've lost father and mother, and I shouldn't like to lose any more of 'em."

"Well, think now," said the Captain; "they're orphans, and I can help them into an asylum, where they will get good clothes and food, and be comfortably cared for and educated." Jim and little Dickie looked with a bewildering sort of state at the good Captain's face, and forthwith they were going into fits of tears.

"O!" said the Captain! "No waterworks, little uns! You'll be able to play with lots of school-fellows, and enjoy yourselves ever so much!"

"Ah!" whimpered Jim, "but we shan't have Bob."

Robert sat very sedate and earnest. He wanted to do what was best; he was thinking of the future of the lads, and desired to do what was wisest for them. His heart was lifted up in a moment to One who has promised to guide us with His counsel, and he seemed braced and strengthened already for a fit reply.

"It will be lone enough here for me, sir," said Bob; "but perhaps it will be quite best for them!"

"Should you mind plenty of sea-room between them and you for a time?" said Captain Summers. Not waiting for Robert's reply, but knocking his idea about being "lone" all over in a minute, he said, "We want you, my boy, to go ABROAD."

Abroad! ah! How the words rang in his ears. How dear even the dingiest places become to us, if they are associated with those we love, and those who have once loved us! The little upper room in Prospect Place seemed very full of beauty just then, in Robert's eyes. It had been the scene of many a little heroic sacrifice on his part of the common good; above all, it was associated with mother-love; you need not wonder, therefore, that Robert looked very pale and thoughtful.

"Well, now; look here, lad," said Captain Summer; "my brother is a merchant at Calcutta, and I promised to send him out a cute youth for his office, if I could find a suitable one, a lad to be trusted; and I think I've found one brisk, and brave too," said the Captain, with a merry sort of chuckle.

"Yes, Robert," said Mr. Fielding. "We never know the power of personal influence, especially of *unconscious*, personal influence. You little knew that I was near you, my boy, when you made the resolve to give the good farmer back his sovereign; and you little thought of the influence that was having on me as a spectator, and so on the whole perhaps of your future life. Trifles are often the turning-points of human history."

Robert looked up into Captain Summer's face, and said with a settled determination, surprising in a lad so young, "It's all right, sir! I'll see the young ones comfortably settled, and I'll be glad to go; that I will sir."

"It will take some time to secure sufficient influence to get both of the little ones into asylums, but I'll manage it, lad," said Captain Summers. "Meanwhile, stick to your block, Bob; stick to your block!"

CHAPTER IV.

BOB SAILS FOR CALCUTTA.

WHEN the captain and Mr. Fielding had gone, Bob sat down and had a hearty good cry. He did not feel ashamed of himself for that. Affairs had taken altogether a new and unexpected turn! He did not wish to stand out against the providence of God. But all who have for the first time felt the sad sensation of an anticipated severance from home, must sympathize with Bob in the pensiveness of his feelings, and the clinging love he had to the poor old tenement which had yet connected with it the endearing associations of home.

In a few moments, however, he began to bestir himself, hastily brushed away his tears, had a good wash, and got ready the tea. After that he became more cheerful, and began to talk about the comforts and pleasure of the prospect before the little lads, in such a way as almost to reconcile little Dick and Jim to the departure of a brother so kind and true to them as brother Bob. "You can play at marbles and tops, too, in the playground," said Robert, "and you'll never be hungry there without having plenty to eat." He then reminded them what the city missionary had told them, that though they were called orphans, they had a Father in heaven who would never leave them nor forsake them. As their custom was, they then all sang a hymn together, and after hearing their little evening prayers, Bob put them into bed, and felt a lighter heart in him than he had done for a long, long time. Often had he looked at those two child-faces asleep, so calm and restful, and said to himself, "If it's a wet, foggy day to-morrow, there'll be few boots to clean, and you'll not get much to eat, little ones;" but now God had been better to him than all his anxieties and fears, and in a spirit of true-hearted gratitude, he thanked God, and took courage.

It is not surprising that a great rush of thoughts came across Robert's mind that night, and that he kept looking at a panorama - not indeed, such a one as he had once seen at the Ragged-school - but a panoramic vision of the future which was now possible to him. He was but a boy after all, and the sense of coming adventure was very pleasant to him.

The preliminaries were in due course arranged: Bob's passage was taken, and his little brothers carefully placed in the asylum. It was, perhaps the most trying moment of his life, when he left them there without being able to speak his good-by, lest he should give way to a flow of tears; he knew that Jim and Dickie would give way too, if he did; so with a cherry wave of the hand, when he was at the gate, they parted.

Robert soon embarked on board the *Speedwell*, for Calcutta. Captain Summers had previously told the Captain, who was an old friend of his, Bob's history; and the

CLEAN YOUR BOOTS, SIR?

CLEAN YOUR BOOTS, SIR?

Captain being naturally interested in him, Bob had, at all events, one friend, and that a most important one, on board - for at sea the Captain is king.

Everything interested Robert in his new life; it was all so fresh to him that his spirits were kept alive by the constant enlivenment of some new discovery; and you needn't wonder that he thought a large East India merchantman the most enjoyable place in the world.

He did not manage at first to make friends with the sailors, though he tried to do so; but they seemed to be taken more with another youth or two who could not only listen to their yarns, but also fall in with all their ways. One incident soon occurred, however, which brought him into a somewhat interesting connection with them. The second mate, named Henry Milcombe, was ill, and his cot was swung in the cuddy, for the sake of air; at eventide it happened that Robert was singing one of the old, well-remembered Ragged-school hymns:

CLEAN YOUR BOOTS, SIR?

"There is a happy land,
　Far, far away;
Where saints in glory stand,
　Bright, bright as day.
Oh! how they sweetly sing,
　Worthy is our Savior King,
Loud let His praises ring!
　Praise, praise for aye.

Come to this happy land,
　Come, come away;
Why will ye doubting stand?
　Why still delay?
Oh! we shall happy be,
When from sin and sorrow free,
Lord, we there shall live with Thee!
　Blest, blest for aye."

It was a calm, still, sunny evening; the prow of the vessel was making that sweet music which in smooth weather always accompanies the dashing aside of the spray, and the setting sun was bathing the ocean in a flood of golden glory.

"What's that?" said the mate.

CLEAN YOUR BOOTS, SIR?

A sailor, who was handing the poor feverish patient a cooling drink, said in his rough way: "It's a lad aboard, as is al'ays at that game of an evening. He's like one of them musical snuff-boxes, when he begins to go you can't stop un nohow."

"I don't want to stop him, Jefferies," said the sick mate: "it sounds sweetly to me. Why, listen - it's what the children of our village used to sing in the vicarage garden on the treat days." And again the low, soft voice of Bob's melody was heard.

"Bright in that happy land
  Beams every eye.
Kept by the Father's hand,
  Love cannot die.
On, then, to glory run,
Be crown and kingdom won,
And, bright above the sun,
  We reign for aye."

"Beautiful!" said the mate. "Why I feel quite a child again myself, Jefferies. What that lad is singing about is what I ought to be thinking about: there's no mistake about that. Go and ask him if he will come speak to me," said the mate.

Robert gladly obeyed the summons, and came close beside the sick man, giving meanwhile an inquisitive glance at his face.

"You're very ill, sir," he said.

"Yes," said the mate; "I'm very, very ill; worse than the doctor thinks I am. I shall never see the dear old country again."

"Perhaps you're making for a better, sir," said Bob. "We may, all of us, go down at sea, and never be heard of more; and it would be sad indeed if we had no home beyond the present world. There's a better country, sir, that is an heavenly."

"I know, I know," said the mate: " I used once to join in the hymn you were just now singing; and it brings back to memory the past; it's just like a smell of meadow hay wafted out to sea from a far-off land, to have all the remembrance of other days brought to one's mind by that hymn. Somehow I have been at home again, sitting by my mother at church, with little sister Mary on the other side."

CLEAN YOUR BOOTS, SIR?

A pleasant conversation followed, and then Robert, in the most natural manner possible, knelt down to pray with him; he prayed for the sick mate's friends, far, far away, and for his own little brothers, thinking, as was natural enough, of Jim and Dickie - but quite ignorant as to who the poor dying mate might be leaving behind him in fatherland and home. One thing, however, was evident, that when Robert was confessing his sin, and craving mercy at the hand of God, the mate said, "Amen!" very earnestly indeed; and his lips moved sometime afterward in secret prayer.

Another conversation followed.

"If you should have to die, sir, are you afraid?" said Bob.

"I know what's right as well as you do," said the mate. "I know all about the Cross of Christ - I've known it from a child; but I've been a bit gay, lately, and I should like to be spared a little longer that I might return to the Lord."

"Turn now, sir," said Robert. "Turn now; I don't know how to talk to such as you, sir," said Bob; "for even concerning salvation, you know about as much as I can tell you. But I remember hearing a good clergyman once say that the love of Christ was like the ocean; you might bring a little cup to the shore every day, and dip into the water; but you could never empty it of its vast supply; and when we think of how many sins we commit every day," said Bob, "we ought to find mighty comfort in those words, 'The blood of Jesus Christ His Son cleanseth us from all sin.' I don't think it's ever too late to come to Christ, sir. And He's waiting at the door of your heart now, sir."

The mate looked at him tenderly, and said, "Thank you, my lad; you've done me good; I feel happier for seeing you. Come again to-morrow."

"But stay," said the mate, leaning on his elbow, and taking a portrait from under his pillow; "Do you know who that is, my lad?"

"It's like enough to you, sir," said Robert. "Perhaps it's your mother."

CLEAN YOUR BOOTS, SIR?

"Yes; my own dear mother," said the mate, "and my sweet little sister's hair is at the back of it. Now promise me, my dear lad," said he, "that if ever you return to dear Old England, you'll visit Clifton, and see them, and tell them all you can about me."

"And that you fell asleep in peace, sir," said Bob.

"In perfect peace," said the mate. "Since yesterday all my resistance to a merciful Saviour has gone, and I feel to rest in the Lord."

Robert's eye brightened. "You love HIM again, sir, now!"

"Yes, my man, I do," he said.

All this time Jefferies, with his bronzed, sea-tanned face, was beside the bed; and he was looking a wee bit uncomfortable at having nothing to do; but he was taking in the whole scene with that kind, appreciative look, which bespoke a hearty English seaman's sympathy and respect.

"We can't afford to lose such as you, sir," said he. "You've been a bit firm and stern, but you've been kind, sir; and they'll miss you for'ards among the crew, as well as abaft among the passengers."

"Take the advice, Jefferies, of a dying man," said the mate. "Seek and serve the Saviour now. It would be sorry work dying, if there was no anchorage for the soul in heaven."

"Ah!" said Jefferies, "it's good soil there, master; the anchor hold taut; don't it, sir. Leastways, the parson said so in the floating chapel in Bristol docks. I didn't forget that."

Not many weeks after, a solemn group might have been seen standing upon the deck at evening; whilst, sinking slowly through the green weaves, out of sight, was the hammock which contained the body of Henry Milcombe, the second mate. Many moist eyes watched the disappearing body, and Robert stood close beside the captain while he read those beautiful words, "I am the resurrection and the life."

Nothing is much more touching than a funeral at sea; all is so solemn and still on deck, and there is the feeling pervading all hearts, that it is a sad and lonely lot to die so far from fatherland and those you love.

After this, many an evening was spent by Robert with the sailors in the forecastle; and he had good reason to know, even before he reached Calcutta, that some who were dissolute, wild, and given to the grossest swearing, had sought and found pardon and life in Jesus Christ. After all, it was but little that he said; but unconscious influence is a stronger power than any of us think, and Robert's whole character and bearing had produced a deep impression on the crew.

At last, after a long sea voyage, the delightful sound of "land in sight!" was heard. The captain had spread out the chart on a table on the poop, and was studying the ship's course, when the man at the masthead again called out, " Land in sight!" Every one instantly wanted to know, where? where?

"On the lardboard bow," was the ready answer. In a few hours the captain took out his glass, and said, "There are the Black Pagodas."

Soon after, the vessel passed the Cuttack coast, a large sand-bank which is skirted with shrub, and the captain looked out for a pilot vessel.

When at last the ship came to an anchor, Robert was much amused with the visit of the trading boats, manned by natives. When these boats were made fast, a brisk sort of traffic commenced, the fruit merchants giving to the sailors bunches of plantains for pieces of soap, etc. Beautiful fruit was brought in for the captain's table; bananas, pamplinos, plantains, and guavas, in abundance. Whilst the trade was going on, Robert was somewhat shocked, in turning his eyes from the richly planted shores, to witness the dreadful spectacle of human bodies floating down the river, whilst on the bodies vultures were seated, quarrelling for the prey, and tearing them to pieces. It is true, indeed, that the Hindoo shasters require that all the dead shall be burned to ashes; but when the relatives are poor, and it is difficult to purchase a certain amount of fuel, they are allowed to put fire on the

CLEAN YOUR BOOTS, SIR?

face, and cast the body into Ganges' stream.

They passed safely the sand-heads, in the mouth of the river Hooghly, and the vessel was soon securely moored. Robert, with the rest of the passengers, was soon rowed by the dinghy-whallahs to shore, and, a stranger in a strange land, had to make the best of his way to the residence of Captain Summer's brother. Robert was much struck by the varied costumes of the motley groups. There were the light dresses, and the scarlet, blue, violet, and pink cummerbunds, or girdles, with which the Mussulman servants were clothed. Then there were the snow-white muslin robes of the pundits, sircars and banyans, contrasting with their swarthy skins.

It was all so unlike the England he had left behind. Here were palanquins, coaches, buggies, and hackeries, all ready for active service. There were the bazaars, too, full of all sorts of Asiatic and European commodities.

Having wandered along the esplanade, adorned with the government house, and many princely residences, perhaps one of the finest promenades in the world, Robert wandered to Chitpore, where the ships of large burden are moored. All these novel scenes helped to divert his mind, and it was astonishing how the bracing air of the voyage, and the feeling of hope concerning his future life, alike helped to lift him above natural feelings of dullness and depression. Alone, he was not alone, for God was with him; and the great Lord over all is rich in mercy to all those who call upon Him, in every island, sea, or shore, over which the blue skies bend; he felt already the meaning of the words, "I will not leave you desolate."

CHAPTER V.

A STRANGE OCCURRENCE.

MR. William Summers gave Bob a kind and Christian welcome. Robert was far too much of a gentleman to presume upon it, and treated his new employer with the greatest possible respect. Mr. Summers placed him in a somewhat arduous post for a youth of seventeen, and watched him, not with the linx-eye of distrust, but with the anxious oversight of a man who particularly wanted in his office somebody whom he could trust. Oh, that one word "Trust!" would that all young people understood half the value of a man who may be put in a place of TRUST!

For the first three years all went on well. Robert had been twice promoted in that short time, and was enjoying, at a very early age, indeed, the respect and confidence of all around him. In the fourth year, however, after his arrival, a very extraordinary affair occurred, which created considerable excitement in mercantile circles in Calcutta, and which greatly affected the position and prospects of Robert Rightheart.

One part of Robert's duty consisted in writing certain orders for the freighting of vessels. These orders were handed over to the shippers; they saw the goods supplied, and three or four months afterwards, Mr. Summers wrote a cheque, payable to the supplier for the freight thus forwarded to some one of the great markets of Europe.

One Tuesday morning, a warehouseman in Calcutta, finding that four months had elapsed, and no cheque had as yet been forwarded, began to be a little inquisitive about it. He had supplied a more than usually costly freight for the English market, and he now began to be anxious to get in his money. Not that he for a moment doubted Mr. Summer's credit.

CLEAN YOUR BOOTS, SIR?

No; his name stood so high that, had it been twenty times as much, he would have had no anxiety. But, truth to tell, he wanted cash just then, and so waited anxiously for the cheque; added to which Mr. Summers was always most punctual in his payments.

No cheque, however, came! He looked over his orders and found the identical one. The name of the vessel was given, and the order for £200 worth of goods was signed in the clear, bold hand of Robert Rightheart.

All this seemed straightforward enough; but when Robert heard of it, after a momentary paleness had passed over him from inward excitement, he asked to see the order. It was produced, and without a moment's hesitation Robert denied that it was his handwriting at all. Unfortunately for him, however, it was so perfect a resemblance that it was almost questionable whether an "expert" would not pronounce it to be his. The consciousness of rectitude sustained him at this terrible crisis in his history; but there were moments when his heart sank within him as he contemplated what might possibly be the issue of the matter.

For the time being, Robert was under a cloud; he never conceived that so complete and clever a forgery could be made; all he felt certain of was this, that the order must have been written by some one who had, for some considerable time, been well acquainted with his hand-writing.

And now some began to look askant at Robert as they passed him in the street; and some few who envied him his success, were heard to say—"he seems a very religious fellow, but look at his morality; they never did think much," they said, "of such steady-going fellows; there was sure to be something wrong with them!"

It is not pleasant to suspect others; but there was a Spaniard in the office who was prejudiced against Robert because he would not consent to receive certain gratuities which went by the name of "eye-blinkers," which were offered to the head clerks, in the shape of perquisites. It was manifest enough what was expected of the receiver; viz., that he should avoid seeing certain irregularities in the shipping of the goods, and that certain maneuverings with them should be allowed to take place without notice or reprimand from the overseeing clerks. Robert refused all such gifts, and the Spaniard had therefore shown spite to Robert in many ways.

Robert felt it wicked to suspect the Spaniard, but what could he do? Mr. Summers had not handed Robert over to the authorities, and he was evidently not in the least shaken in his good opinion of him; but others were, and it was a matter of the highest moment that his character should be cleared at the earliest possible opportunity.

As Robert pondered and prayed over the matter, he remembered distinctly that he had seen a swarthy, low-browed, doubtful-looking man, walking with the same Spaniard, months ago, in the old China bazaar.

Robert could not sleep. He used to rise very early to read a portion from the word of God, which has some promises for every hour of need; he lighted upon one passage which greatly cheered him, and which he perused again and again; "He shall bring forth thy righteousness as the light, and thy judgment as the noonday." That was indeed like a voice from heaven, speaking to his soul. It was enough. It gave him rest and strength. Greater was He that was for him, than any that could be against him. Robert felt sure of that; and none but those who have passed through such a season of tribulation can understand how, amid all failing sources of comfort, there is One that never fails! The loving sympathy of Jesus Christ is the same yesterday, to-day, and for ever.

Mr. Summers, as was to be expected, declined to pay the amount, and in the course of time the matter was duly brought before a court of law.

The evening before the trial, Robert tapped at Mr. Summer's private office door, and heard the well-known, quick response, "Come in!"

"Would you oblige me, sir," said Robert, "by permitting me again to inspect the written order to which my name is subscribed?"

"Most certainly," said Mr. Summers; "and now, Mr. Rightheart, whoever suspects you of forgery and fraud, remember this — although this is a mysterious case, I never for one moment have suspected you. I did not doubt your word at the time; neither, remember do I now."

A flush came over Robert's brow; he felt as if he must hold the office-table or fall; but the excitement, which visibly shook his whole frame, passed away. It was a deep feeling of gratitude both to God and man, such as few occasions in life can call forth — gratitude to God for sustaining his faith and trust, and gratitude to Mr. Summers for giving him so cheering an expression of confidence previous to the approaching hour of trial.

Robert took the order in his hand and turned it this way and that, upside and down; but the more he examined it, the more startled he was at the free and easy way in which his signature had been copied; there was not one artificial line or break in the whole.

As, however, he carefully examined the order, he made a discovery which made him flush, perhaps deeper crimson than he had done just before—his color came and went—and his heart beat so violently that it shook his whole frame; however, he waited for the morrow, and kept quiet concerning a matter which might help him in the eventful hour.

CHAPTER VI.

THE TRIAL.

AS you may suppose, the courthouse was very crowded indeed. Robert was held in high respect among the merchants and civilians generally, in Calcutta. He might many times have greatly increased his salary by leaving Mr. Summers, but he had considered it only right to remain faithful to the brother of one who had lifted him out of his shoeblack life, and sent him so kindly to the Indies.

As the time approached, the interest and excitement greatly increased. Crowds waited outside to know what turn the tide of affairs was taking, and the feeling of high-wrought expectation told even upon the usually quiet denizens at Howrah.

The judge took his seat; several matters of detail were first disposed of, and then the merchant put in his claim for the £200, so that only indirectly was it a trial of poor Robert.

As the trial went on, several witnesses were examined without much light being thrown on the affair.

It was asked whether that was the usual way in which Mr. Rightheart wrote the order — whether it would not be better to have printed ones, signed by the merchant only — whether all the writing as well as the signature was in Mr. Rightheart's handwriting?

The signature appeared indeed to be so; and there was apparently nothing wrong in the order. It was handed from the bench to the counsel, and from one counsel to another who turned it this way and that, scrutinizing it in the closest possible manner.

The merchant said he did not wish in any way to injure Mr. Rightheart, but he asked significantly, what *was* he to do? The

CLEAN YOUR BOOTS, SIR?

goods had been *bona fide* sent, and were without doubt by this time turned into cash.

The judge presently asked quietly, "Who brought you this order?" He did not know. It was left at his office in his absence—he was so accustomed to such orders, signed by Mr. Rightheart, that it never struck him to note very closely the order-bringer; he thought it was all right, as all the rest had been, and so he shipped the goods.

The case seemed to be hopelessly inexplicable, when Mr. Rightheart, who was not there as a criminal, it being a simple case of suing for money over-due, was allowed without opposition to give evidence.

Previously to arriving at the court-house, Robert had made a few inquiries, which we shall presently see the value of. There was quite a buzz of excited conversation as he stepped briskly into the witness-box, which was succeeded by a stillness like death. When he proceeded to give his evidence, the whole assembly was filled with eager interest.

It was Robert's turn to speak now — and he meant to throw a little light upon matters, if he could; but though he was brave, and knew that he was honest, you need not wonder very much that he heard his own heart beating when he first commenced to give evidence before the court. Even then he lifted up his heart to Him who judgeth righteously, who is in this peculiar sense the God of the orphan, and who seeth not as man seeth! A seeming trifle had enabled Robert, if not thoroughly to solve the mystery, at all events to clear himself. How could he be sufficiently grateful for that!

When the order was handed up to Robert in the course of his examination, he handed it respectfully back to the bench, and said, "Will your lordship allow me to ask you attention to the paper on which the order is written?"

The judge held it steadily before him.

"If you will lift it up to the light," said Robert, "you will see a water-mark on it,

CLEAN YOUR BOOTS, SIR?

THE TRIAL. Page 76.

and the maker's name." A visible thrill ran across the faces of the spectators.

"Perhaps your lordship will ask Mr. Summers if we ever use this paper?" said Mr. Rightheart.

Mr. Summers seemed struck as with a sudden surprise himself. How stupid of him not to have noticed this before! "Certainly not," said he, " we always use the same maker's paper, and it is not this."

"Where is this paper sold?" said the judge.

"Only at one house in Calcutta," said Robert, "and the tradesman who retails it is here."

"Let him step up," said the judge. The following colloquy then took place:

"Do you sell much of this paper?"

"Not much."

"Have you sold any lately?"

"Well, we sold off our last quantity about four months ago; in fact, I remember parting with the last package of it."

"To whom?" said the judge. "Can you remember to whom? Now, consider what you say. It is of immense importance to a

CLEAN YOUR BOOTS, SIR?

young man present here, and you are bound in honor to afford us all the evidence you can. I must caution you against the crime of suppressing truth."

There was a positive tremor in the court, an awful stillness in which men could almost hear, not only the beating of their own, but the beating of each other's hearts; a silence that might indeed be felt; for on this witness evidently depended the issue of the whole case.

When the name fell from the lips of the witness, there was such a scene in court as had not been witnessed for many a long, long day; for the witness named, distinctly enough for all to hear, the Spaniard in Mr. Summer's office.

The crowd did not stay to think what an awful charge would thus be brought against the Spaniard; they remembered only Mr. Rightheart, and they raised such a stout-lunged cheer, and such cheers upon cheers as never before had been heard in the quiet precincts of that legal chamber. No usher of any court could suppress such shouts as those. Robert was literally carried away upon the shoulders of the spectators straight up to the office of Mr. Summers, where a perfect ovation awaited him. After a time, Robert asked to be permitted, having passed through a scene so exciting, and on which, as he well knew, all his future history hung, to be permitted to have an hour or two to himself. It need not be told that, when left alone, he turned his first thought to Him who maketh the storm a calm, and who ordereth all our ways. God had not forgotten him, and now with a glad and grateful heart he knelt down to pour forth the old and inspired thanksgiving to God, — "Bless the Lord, O my soul, and forget not all His benefits."

CHAPTER VII.

THE RETURN TO ENGLAND.

WE need not delay this history with any account of the trial of the Spaniard; nor need we inquire concerning his guilty companion in the plot, by whose agency the goods were turned into cash at the English port, save to say that he managed to escape with the booty, whilst the Spaniard was condemned to a long period of servitude for his sin. We are of course mainly interested in the fortunes of Robert Rightheart, who from that day, dated a new era in his existence. He was honored in the city and promoted in his house of business, until, alike to his surprise and joy, Mr. Summers communicated to him the pleasing intelligence that he had determined to offer him the position of junior partner in the concern. There are moments in most lives, when all the channels of the heart seem full; when long cherished hopes are unexpectedly fulfilled; and there are moments, too, when what could scarcely be called hopes, but rather dreams of the fancy, are, after years of hard, earnest toil, turned into realities. Not often indeed so early as was the case with Robert Rightheart. Alas! that so often in this world advancement comes when those whose faces would so have brightened at the intelligence are sleeping in the dust. What a day would it have been for mother or father, if to those humble lodgings could have been conveyed the news, "Your boy is partner in an East India house!" But God's ways are wiser than ours; and perhaps this would have been too much for the character of Robert Rightheart to bear.

It was with a strange sense of his new importance that he now attended office, and commenced to mingle in the best circles of society. He was, however, too

CLEAN YOUR BOOTS, SIR?

well taught in God's word to have his heart lifted up. He knew full well that power cometh from God only; that he putteth down one and setteth up another; and, amidst all the favors of men, he never neglected to seek that favor which cometh from God only. Hence the hand of the Lord was with him.

The business of the house was greatly augmented through the activity and energy of Robert Rightheart; and it soon became necessary for one of the partners to visit England and arrange for a great increase of trade, and for a better representation of their house in the city of London. It was determined that Robert Rightheart should go, remain three months in his native land, and then return to Calcutta.

We need not detail the varied incidents of Robert's voyage home, nor stay to picture those quiet evening hours, in which, with the bright stars above him and the deep sea everywhere around him, he went on deck to meditate upon his outward voyage, and to consider the wonderful loving-kindness of his God. It would be impossible to describe his mingled feelings when once again he saw the white cliffs of dear Old England — those cliffs he had watched with dewy eyes as the vessel took him out to Calcutta, fortuneless, but not friendless. How different was his position now! His heart filled with strangely conflicting emotions as he remembered what fatherly care God had taken of the poor orphan lad who put his youthful trust in Him.

The vessel hove to in sight of Dover, on a Saturday morning. Robert was soon conveyed, with other of his fellow-passengers, by boat to the harbor, and then proceeded by the next express train to London Bridge. When he arrived he could scarcely realize that the city was the same place, and that he was the same person; that voyage to India seemed to have severed his history into two distinct parts. Perhaps the most interesting episode of that day, after all, was that in which, after coming up King William Street, he crossed over to the old familiar spot where he once bent over his work as one of the "Red Brigade" of boot-cleaning boys! His feelings nearly overcame him. As he pondered on the past, little pieces of his almost forgotten self met him and moved him one after another—trifling incidents which had happened there kept leaping up in his mind like trout in a stream. As memory carried on its interesting work, he became slowly lost to all his surrounding objects, and, as the tears rolled down his face, he was lifting up his heart to God in gratitude and joy. Presently he stepped to the back of the statue, and ere had time to fix his eye on the old familiar spot where he once earned his daily pence, a sharp, clear, ringing voice, like what his own used to be, cried out,

"Clean your boots, sir?"

Fancy that! Almost involuntarily he obeyed; placed his foot—the young India merchant's foot—upon the block, and watched the lad with intense interest and earnestness as he polished away at his boot.

CLEAN YOUR BOOTS, SIR?

As soon as his feelings were sufficiently calmed down, with great quietness of tone, he said, "I used to clean boots here, my lad."

"You, sir!"

"Yes; when I was sixteen years old, and I am three and twenty now."

"Just about seven years ago, that is, sir. My eye! You're joking, ain't you, sir?"

"No; I cleaned boots upon this very spot."

"And you're a gentleman now, sir," giving as he spoke, a glance at his face and form.

"I hope so."

"Had a fortune left you, sir?"

"No, my lad."

"Worked your way up, sir?"

"Yes, my lad. Look here, remember this: you do your best where you are, and that will fit you for doing something better when God shows the way; and there are golden opportunities in most people's lives."

And so, dropping a bright new sixpence into the lad's hand, Mr. Rightheart

CLEAN YOUR BOOTS, SIR?

journeyed on his way. The old Prospect Place he found was gone forever, so it was not of any use this walking to that scene of other days. The underground railway had passed through the neighborhood, demolishing that and many such-like places. Prospect Place now only existed in the memory of those who once toiled and suffered there.

But Jim and Dickie were living and doing well. The elder boy had left the asylum, and Captain Fielding had got him a clerkship in the London and County bank. Thither Robert wended his way, and soon glimpsed his brother just leaving office for the Saturday half-holiday. It was the same broad, bonnie face, but how altered the figure and the form! Robert touched him on the shoulder, and said, "Jimmy, boy!" and in an instant they were in each other's embrace.

Sunday morning came, and Robert woke up in his well-appointed bedroom in the Railway hotel, and, after breakfast, hastened off to the house of God. After he had dined he made ready for another expedition. He was longing to pay a visit to the dear old ragged school. Yes! amid all the city improvements, that, thank God, was standing yet; what was better than all, it was still prospering, and had been greatly enlarged. As he approached the place he saw some little urchins wending their way up the dark passage leading to the old familiar white-washed schoolroom, and Mr. Rightheart followed in their wake.

The door was now opened, and quite a buzz was heard, as of so many busy bees round and about their hives. A little bell, however, presently tinkled, and silence was secured — at least such silence as can at the best be secured in a school of wandering City Arabs, such as ragged schools contain. After the opening prayer, the president gave out a hymn, and two or three teachers commenced to gather together their classes. Robert Rightheart entered the room quietly and quite unobtrusively. One look at that venerable form in the desk assured him that he saw before him his own dear old president.

CLEAN YOUR BOOTS, SIR?

Deeply moved by all the recollections of that school, where he had first heard the name of Jesus, and learned to put his young heart's trust in him, Robert yet resolved to play the man. He went up, shook his old teacher cordially and respectfully by the hand, and announced himself the little Bob of earlier years. After mutual recognition and conversation, the president asked Robert if, as soon as the lessons were over, he would kindly say a word to the assembled children. The impression made by that brief, but earnest address, was never lost. Robert reminded them that each one of them might enjoy a happiness such as this world can never give, viz., joy in God through Jesus Christ; and then he went on to assure them that success is not to be measured by what we attain, but by what we are; and that to be faithful and true in any station to which it may please God in his providence to call us, is the wise ambition of all those who would be brave and true disciples of Christ. "At the same time," said he, with peculiar emphasis, "never forget that God does bless industry, temperance, self-denial, and earnestness."

He then very modestly told the simple story of his own life. It was a scene never to be forgotten, and more than one heart was, on that very day, dedicated to the Saviour. It was very evident that Robert was not at all ashamed of his early connection with the ragged school; he did not try to be considered a great man by the difficult and foolish process of trying to leave the beginnings of his life to oblivion; he was ready to confess his humble origin, and to extol the goodness of God. He thus became as much honored for his manliness as he was happy in possessing a sense of self-respect. Of one thing too, he was determined; — he never, at home or abroad, would be ashamed of the Gospel of Jesus Christ, for he had found in Christ a friend that sticketh closer than a brother. The gospel made him what he was—he was sure of that.

CHAPTER VIII.

MARY MILCOMBE AND THE MARRIAGE DAY.

WE have now to turn to the meeting which next day took place between Robert and his friend Captain Summers. That gentleman was still hale and well, and had been rejoiced to hear from time to time of the prosperity and progress of his young friend, the little shoe-black boy. As for Mr. Fielding, as may be supposed, he was in a flutter of expectation when he heard of the anticipated arrival in England of the little lad he had been the instrument, in the hands of God, of lifting to a higher level than even he himself had ventured to suppose was possible.

CLEAN YOUR BOOTS, SIR?

Early on the Monday morning Robert rose early, left his hotel before breakfast, and got to the Fieldings' house just as family worship was about to commence. He lifted his hand to raise the knocker, but Mr. Fielding had caught sight of him coming up the garden path, and hastened to open the door himself—he willingly gave that honor to Robert—and a welcome more kind, Christian, and affecting, was never given on this earth than that which Mr. Fielding gave to the lad whom he had befriended in the beginning of his history, and who looked up to him with respect and gratitude, and with the joy of a successful man.

You may judge how solemn and tender was the service of the family altar that morning. They first sang the hymn—

"God moves in a mysterious way,
  His wonders to perform;
He plants his footsteps in the sea,
  And rides upon the storm."

CLEAN YOUR BOOTS, SIR?

Then, after the reading of a psalm of thanksgiving, and the offering of prayer, they took their places at the cheerful breakfast-table, where questions came in so thick and fast on Robert Rightheart, that it seemed at first doubtful whether he would get any breakfast at all. But as he was soon led to promise to spend a week with them, the quick firing of the questions gave place to exclamation of "That's capital," from the younger branches of the family, and with such remarks as, "You'll tell us all about it this evening, Mr. Rightheart, won't you." So you need not wonder that, both in the business he had in hand at the City, and in what the South Sea islanders call a "Talkee, talkee," at home, Robert found himself in full employ. A happy week it was. Robert had no need to invent tales to amuse them, for his experience of life in India had furnished him with quite a panorama of illustrations.

After spending the first week under Mr. Fielding's roof, Robert remembered that he had a promised duty to perform connected with the desire of the mate who died on his outward voyage to Calcutta. Having obtained the address of the mother, he started at once for Clifton, and reached Bristol by the afternoon express.

His cab was some half hour afterwards sounding its gritty way up the gravel drive which led to a sweet, secluded house on the downs, close to the most beautiful parts of the romantic scenery of Clifton. As he sat looking out of the parlor window on the lawn where the shadows of the trees were falling on the garden path, he saw the approaching figure of a lady, whose features at once told him that she was the mother of the poor mate who had passed to glory so far away from that dear home! True, six or seven years had elapsed, and the mother's grief had become somewhat softened, but there was a pensiveness about her brow which spoke of the abiding memory of the boy she had loved so well. She was not ignorant concerning the name on the card which the servant took from Robert. No! She had heard from the chief mate of the ship about

CLEAN YOUR BOOTS, SIR?

Robert's tender, Christian kindness to her son — and naturally enough, she had long desired to see his face. Often had she, with a fervent heart, thanked God for raising up such a friend out at sea for her only son — and she had now the opportunity of expressing, in her poor way, her gratitude to Robert Rightheart. With a trembling step she came down the garden walk — for now that she was about to welcome him — memories of the past crowded back upon her heart, and the excitement was almost too much for the shattered frame to bear. Dear gray motherhood, how beautiful thou art! It has been well said, "We can only have one mother," and there are few sorrows deeper or more permanent than the sorrow of a mother for the loss of her only son.

The effort must however be made, and Mrs. Milcombe was too brave a woman to succumb. She entered the room where Robert was; her thin, white lips trembled, but she could not speak. Robert understood her emotion, quietly took her hand in his and sat beside her; thus for some time they remained until Robert, with quiet gentleness of manner, ventured to touch upon the subject which he well knew was better spoke of than suppressed. He did it with such genuine sincerity, and such delicate courtesy of manner, that the mother's heart seemed all at rest while he was speaking. She now heard for the first time the full story of her boy's confidence in the Friend of sinners, and of the sweet peace which rested on his heart, as he went through the valley of the shadow of death, fearing no evil. In the gathering twilight they were still talking on, when the door gently opened, and the evening light fell upon a face of one who had enough in her features to show that she was sister to the dead mate; and yet there was in the face, a lofty, intellectual cast, which did not belong to his. She had the highest type of beauty, a kind and gentle eye, with a mystically thoughtful face, over which her golden hair fell in massive tresses. It was not that her eye was blue so much as that it was thoughtful, which made her the lovely girl she was. Her age was just nineteen;

CLEAN YOUR BOOTS, SIR?

the little girl that her poor brother had left in short dresses, playing with the doll, was now in the early blossom of womanly beauty; not fairer however to look upon than she was fair in character. Many a poor woman in the dark courts of the neighboring Bristol could tell how Mary Milcombe had made the valley of sorrow look beautiful, by bringing to them the message of the Saviour's peace; and many a broken prayer went to heaven with her name whispered in it, as asking a blessing upon her labor of love. Many an eye glanced back at her, as she passed, basket in hand, to take some delicacies and comforts to the homes of the poverty stricken and the sick; and it seemed quite natural to the good people to think and speak of her as some angel of mercy passing by.

Robert was not free from the impressibility of nature which most young men of his age might be expected to feel in the presence of a girl as Mary Milcombe; he was certainly conscious as she entered the room that he had never seen any face so thoughtful and beautiful before.

Robert needed no pressing to remain a few days with them at Clifton—and the days were rapidly gliding into weeks. He had many duties to discharge in London, but he easily persuaded himself that it was not so very fatiguing to go to the metropolis by express one day and back by the express the next evening! He certainly did not neglect his work. He was more fortunate than he expected in planning for an increase of London accommodation for his firm; and he impressed all who came into connection with him that he was not one who made religion a stalking-horse to deceive, but a truthful and upright man.

The month that Robert had spent at Mr. Milcombe's had been a peculiarly pleasant one. His heart had not been taken captive at once, but the more he saw of the graces of Mary's character, the more he was drawn towards her. It soon appeared that the appreciation and affection were mutual, and it became whispered in the vicinity that Mary Milcombe was engaged.

CLEAN YOUR BOOTS, SIR?

"Engaged is her?" said a poor old sick body in one of the visitation districts which Mary weekly took. "Engaged! God bless her! But what's to become of we?"

Ah! many a poor creature asked in heart that simple question—"What's to become of we?" And if "a good name is rather to be chosen than great riches, and loving favor before silver or gold," Mary was rich indeed, for her name had become a household word in many a poor man's house.

Mrs. Milcombe may be forgiven the tears which she shed when she thought upon the long, long distance that would henceforth separate her daughter from her; but they were to return in a few years; that was one spring of comfort; and if she was taken away, as soon indeed she must be by death, with whom could she leave her daughter with more confidence than she could in the care of one so brave and kind and true as Robert Rightheart? So she bravely bore up after her first discomposure of mind concerning the separation, and surrendered her dear child with her best blessing to the once shoe-black boy.

The wedding-day at last drew near, and all was arranged concerning the presence of Mr. Fielding, Captain Summers, and other friends. It was a fine sight. Robert Rightheart, with his erect and manly form, and his beautiful bride leaning on his arm, came forth from the church, surrounded by something better than a crowd of mere holiday sight-seers. Yes; true friends were those who had helped Robert on when none beside befriended him; and true friends these also from the abodes of poverty, who had stitched some bit of bright ribbon on to a faded bonnet, to be as fresh as possible when they came to strew a few flowers in the path, and to send up earnest prayers to God for a blessing on the bride, who had so often cheered the weary, desolate homes of the fatherless and the widow.

Ring merrily, ye bells, from the tall church tower amid the green trees yonder. It is a happy day indeed for Robert

CLEAN YOUR BOOTS, SIR?

Rightheart; and those who know his bride best, say, that her price is beyond rubies.

We need not describe the scene at the marriage breakfast, nor the group on the lawn, as the carriage drove from that picturesque home. No; we will only invite the reader to one scene more.

The bride and bridegroom had arrived in London, and spent some days in its vicinity, when, one afternoon, as they passed near the Exchange, Mary said, "Remember your promise, Robert."

Yes; there they stood—this happy pair—the East Indian merchant and his fair young wife, close to the spot so remarkable in Robert's history.

"A shilling all around!" What did it mean? The boys could scarcely believe their eyes. "This here's the gent as once cleaned boots here," said the boy to whom Robert, at his last visit, had told the fact.

"Is it you, sir? Hurray!" said the smallest lad of the lot. "Hurray!" and all the boys took the back of their brushes and gave the old till-lill-lill-la for joy.

CLEAN YOUR BOOTS, SIR?

A word or two of quiet talk to them, and as customers were coming up, he and his wife went on their way; not so quickly, however, but that Robert heard yet once again the old, familiar sound, "Clean your boots, sir?"

CHAPTER IX.

ROBERT'S HOME IN CALCUTTA.

WHEN Robert returned to Calcutta with his bride, he enjoyed the welcome back of a large circle of friends, and those tokens of respect which his well-tested character had earned. He was a successful man, and success has its dangers as well as its delights. Many are faithful to Christ in adversity whose love waxes cold toward Him in prosperity. Many a beautiful plant that has battled bravely with the wind and hail of spring-time, is scorched and dried up by the glaring heat of summer. Robert knew the only source of safety, and sought the protecting shadow of the Most High. The glare of success did not therefore blind him to his duties as a Christian citizen; he took a great interest in the missionary operations that were so successfully going on in Calcutta, and in all such enterprises of love he was stimulated and helped by his faithful and devoted wife.

No step in life is of such vast importance as that momentous one of marriage. In that relationship we either lift each other up to heaven, or drag each other down from the holy elevation of character. We either clog the wheels of duty's chariot, or else we speed the steeds thereof on their way.

Robert and his wife were helpers of each other's joy, and were never happier than when they were devising some new plan of usefulness, or showing loving sympathy to those who were sore harassed and overburdened in the Great Master's work. Not long after their return to Calcutta, they were visiting at the house of a fashionable friend; and as they were sitting at dessert, with all the choice fruits of the country before them, oranges, limes, plantains, custard-apples, and such other luxuries as crowd an eastern table, the conversation turned to the Christian schools that had been established for native children, and to mission work in general. An officer who was present, said, in a satirical, off-hand way, that it was a work started by a few fanatics, who were likely enough to cause another revolt in time, and to raise the deadly enmity of the natives. "See," said he, "how futile the work is; here we have many varied fruits suited to various shores, and so we have religions suited to various peoples. What is the use of disturbing them, eh?"

Mr. Rightheart quietly asked him what he thought, not only of their godlessness, but of the cruel rites practised at the Churruck Poojah festival, and of the abominations of Suttee, where the living widow was burned with the dead husband, and of the car festival, when the air is rent with cries of "Jye Juggernaut! Victory to Juggernaut!" while dead and mangled bodies are left behind of men and women who have cast themselves beneath the wheels. "Now, sir," said Mr. Rightheart, addressing the officer, "those are all *fruits* before you, all sweet, luscious, pleasant, refreshing; and I admit that God suits special fruits to special places. But these false religions are poison-plants, sir. They poison the health, they poison the home-happiness, they poison the conscience with opiates, they poison the immortal soul!

As to missionary work, sir," he further said "permit me to remind you of what that great staff officer said, whose opinion will surely have weight with you, I mean the Duke of Wellington. When some visitor of his found fault with missionaries as unsettling men's minds in India, and asked him what he thought of the enterprise? 'Think, sir; think sir;' the great duke answered; 'They can do no other, sir; They've got their marching orders, sir, "Go you into all the world and preach the gospel to every creature.' "And certainly," said Mr. Rightheart, "I cannot understand any one seeing how idolatry has cursed India, not wishing the missions and the schools a most divine success. With all my heart I do." In these days it wants much

CLEAN YOUR BOOTS, SIR?

courage for Christians to speak so plainly; but years ago, under the rule of the Hon. East India Company, it was in the highest degree unpopular, in what was called good society, to plead for missions.

The officer was not only effectually silenced, but in his heart of hearts he felt a respect for the man who could thus, at a friend's table, brave every one's opinion and dare to speak the convictions of his conscience! We are never so mistaken as when we think that it is wisest to accommodate ourselves to our company, and to "do at Rome as the Romans do," as the old, oft-quoted proverb expresses it. We should remember that the man who leaves his Christianity behind him when he enters un-Christian society, has very little Christianity indeed to lose, and is a time-server instead of a servant of Christ.

Robert and his wife found many pleasures in their Eastern life of a healthy and innocent kind. Especially did they enjoy the cool morning of India. They used to rise very early indeed, and as soon as the morning gun was fired, which occurred the moment the first gleam of light appeared in the horizon, the syces saddled the horses, and the voice of the sirdar-bearer at their chamber-door announced the morning hour. Then, quickly ready, they mounted for their enjoyable ride, and then started forth, passing underneath the tall bamboos which overarched their path; and then by the elegant palm-trees, with the luxuriant creeper in full blossom around them; occasionally they saw some skulking jackals returning to the jungle after the depredations of the night; they would pass temples containing large idols for worship, paddy-fields where men and women knee-deep in water were planting rice; then an elephant bearing a burden of boughs and branches, and brushing the flies from its side with one carried in its trunk; then rich, green groves composed of mangoe-trees. And now, as they ride forward, what is the man doing in the distance? See, he rises and lies down, rises and lies down, at every step. Alas! he is a deluded idolater; he is measuring the road from his native

CLEAN YOUR BOOTS, SIR?

village to Juggernaut's temple, by the length of his body; he carries an iron nail in his hand, and scratches the ground as far as he can reach, then puts his foot to the mark, and scratches it again. And now, under the shade of the tamarind-trees, Mr. and Mrs. Rightheart rest their horses, and then ride home. After that, the duties of the day must be discharged within the cool shade of office or house, until restful evening comes.

The year after their return to Calcutta was marked by the birth of a bonnie boy, and the succeeding summer a sweet little daughter was born to them. Home became doubly blessed, and it was the delight of their parents to watch them as gifts from Him for whom they must one day give account. The little ones had many escapes from danger, the most notable of which was that of little Robert, who, on one occasion, when his father was in the verandah, came trotting along to him from the garden riding upon a piece of old bamboo, which the little one had picked up somewhere about. Suddenly the child dashed it from him and uttered a loud scream. The cause of his terror was not long a secret, for out of the bamboo came a young cobra capella snake, about a foot and a half long; but, though alarmed, the child providentially was not bitten, and the reptile was soon destroyed. Some such early dangers the children met with, but the most amusing of all these escapades was that of precious little Maude, who, when two years old, was in the nurse's arms one day as she was carrying in some plantains to be eaten at tiffin; a monkey, who had been perched upon an almond-tree, quietly leaped down, took a circuitous route, and seized the plantains from behind. The ayah battled for a moment, but Jacko got the best of it and bore the plantains off in triumph.

The little ones became much attached to this Christian ayah, who took a nurse's care of them, and watched the opening of their earliest thought. What servants can do for good, only the great day of eternity will reveal. This ayah tried to take the tendrils of those young hearts and entwine

CLEAN YOUR BOOTS, SIR?

them around the cross of Christ, and it seemed as though she would be well rewarded for her pains. She loved them as her own; she had been with them from the beginning,; and she loved to hear them, in the broken speech of infancy, saying, "Gentoo Jesus," at her knees at eventide.

But sorrows come to every home, and none are exempt; the shadow of a great grief now settled over this peaceful family. Little Maude fell sick of fever, and though all that medical skill could do was done for her, she drooped and drooped, and died. Oh, how the mother's heart ached with grief! She had longed that her own dear mother in England might see her beautiful babes and be happy at the sight. None can tell but those separated by the wide, wide sea how she had pictured the time when the child's little, soft hand would entwine itself with the gray locks of a beloved grandmamma. But it was not so to be. The mother pressed the marble cheek with kisses, but could not wake it up to life. The child-spirit had passed to the better land, that world where the small and the great are gathered together, and where death shall be no more; where the ransomed souls of children are for ever praising that dear Saviour, who, when upon this earth, took little children in His arms and blessed them, as he said "Suffer the little children to come unto me, and forbid them not, for of such is the kingdom of heaven."

This was the first heavy trouble that Mr. Rightheart and his young wife were called upon to pass through; but God gave them grace to bear it, and to recover strength before another trial came. A dark cloud was indeed rising on the edge of the horizon, and as yet they saw it not. In great mercy it was concealed from them at the time; but He who sees the end from the beginning, Himself saw its advent, and prepared them for its coming. A panic of unprecedented character came over the commercial world — one more severe and shaking than any that had yet occurred; and so depreciated did the property become which Robert's firm held, that for the time being they thought that all was

CLEAN YOUR BOOTS, SIR?

over with their fortunes. Mr. Rightheart returned one sad evening to his home with his forehead shadowed with care, and his heart heavy with anxiety; the quick eye of his wife detected that there was something seriously wrong, and she quietly took his hand in hers and sat down beside him. "Mary," said he, when he could speak, "can you bear to hear that we are ruined?—Yes, ruined—if no change takes place before to-morrow—we are ruined, dear!"

"RUINED, Robert!" she said, her eyes filled with tears; "No, never, dear! Your character and reputation are not gone, my love; and as long as we preserve a conscience void of offence toward God and toward men, we never can be ruined. We are rich in each other's love, and rich in the help of our Redeemer, and we need fear no evil; for is it not said, 'All things work together for good to them that love God?' Do you not remember, Robert," she continued, "telling me how little you expected in early days all the rich mercies which surround you? God gave, and God can take away, as He did with our own dear Maude; and what is all our property compared to her? Let us have faith in God. Ruined! Never, love," she said. "We are rich in what we *are*, not in what we *have*."

These words fell like dew on Robert's parched heart; he had felt far more for his gentle wife, unaccustomed as she was to poverty or trial, than he had for himself; and now to hear such brave, inspiring words from her filled his heart with joy, and nerved him for all the anxieties of his future lot.

In a few days, Calcutta friends surrounded him, whose names would have been a tower of strength to any man; every acceptance was honored; and though he and his partners lost much in the depreciated value of goods, and the inability of many to pay their accounts, yet they weathered the storm. They came forth with weakened fortunes, but with spotless reputation; and Robert, chastened by trial, was more determined than ever to live, not unto himself, but unto Him that died for him, and rose again. Tribulation

CLEAN YOUR BOOTS, SIR?

drew him closer than ever to Christ, and many of the hymns he had learned in the ragged school came now with living power and energy to his heart, proving that seed once sown springs up in many after-harvest times to the good of man and the glory of God.

We must leave Robert and his future enterprises now. We have recorded enough to show that life is not an unbroken history of success; that however sunny for the most part it may be, that yet clouds and darkness will come over many of its fairest, gladdest scenes; and that however faithful we may be to duty and God, we cannot, as some of the old story books used to say of their heroes, expect to live happily afterwards all the days of our lives. No, there is a cross in every lot; there is a constant need for dependence upon Divine grace, and for submission to that Divine will which alike casts us down and lifts us up again. Successful men have their peculiar dangers and their secret cares. The heroism and energy of Robert Rightheart could not free him from the earthly lot of man; tribulation and trial commingled with all our earthly joys, and bereavement darkens our brightest days! Although, however, love to Christ will not free us from tribulation, it will enable us to endure it as seeing Him who is invisible.

We could not, therefore, end this history of Robert Rightheart without giving a place in our closing chapters to his early sorrows. We must leave him now and his future where we must all leave our own, in the hands of that Redeemer who rules over all. We must not, however, forget to remark, that true Christian heroism is its own reward, and that had no glorious future of earthly victory opened up before Robert in this world, yet that, earnest and faithful, he would always have enjoyed the happiness of a heart at peace with God, and the consciousness of endeavors to do His will. We are not permitted to look forward to success as the necessary reward of duty, as though it were a law without exception; it is true that godliness is profitable for all things, having the promise of the life that now is as well as of

CLEAN YOUR BOOTS, SIR?

that which is to come; but it is also true that God may see fit to withhold outward good, and that we ought to be faithful unto death whatever may be our lot.

Many things the history of Robert Rightheart has taught us. We should be fearless amid the scorn of companions for doing right, as he was on the day when they ridiculed him for giving the "old un" back his money. We should honor our parents, as he did; tenderly and unselfishly did he make up his little store and care for his poor paralyzed father. We should be like him in his love and loyalty to the Saviour, as witnessed in his first voyage out; and in fidelity to our employers, as manifested in his clerkship in the East India firm. We need not leave the record of his history without resolves to be like him. We may never don the uniform of a shoe-black boy, but we may all wear the garment of his goodly character, and bear about with us the same sword of the Spirit, the word of God. When next we hear the now familiar sound, "Clean your boots, sir?" and turn our head to glance at the

CLEAN YOUR BOOTS, SIR?

face of the little lad, who has from morn to eve the task of brightening boots, it may not be amiss to ask ourselves if we boys and girls put as much energy into our school work as he does into the business of his block. See how carefully he goes to work about it, how he brushes your trouser leg, then turns it back, then squares your foot properly on the box then blacks and brightens, blacks and brightens, till he gets the finest polish that he can. Yes, that's the style! Better and better, boys! Better and better, girls!

"Clean your boots, sir? Here you are, sir!" Both hands, earnestly; that's it! And whether you pay him more or less, he has done his work well; he has put CONSCIENCE even into that boot-blacking business; so do you into yours. Do your work well, for its own sake, whatever it may be; and as you pass on out of the cheerful sound of "Clean your boots, sir?" remember one thing more from Robert Rightheart's history; namely, this, that the soldiers of Christ wear many outward uniforms, and

CLEAN YOUR BOOTS, SIR?

that it is possible to be faithful to Him in whatever position our lot may be cast.

*"And whatever ye do, do it heartily, as to the
Lord, and not unto men,
Knowing that of the Lord ye shall receive the
reward of the inheritance;
for ye serve the Lord Jesus Christ.
Moreover, it is required in stewards, that a
man be found faithful.*

*I Corinthians, iv.2
Colossians, iii.23,24.*

The End.

Lamplighter Rare Collector's Series

The Basket of Flowers. CHRISTOPH VON SCHMID
First written in the late seventeen or early eighteen hundreds, this book is the first in the **Lamplighter Collector's Series** which gave birth to Lamplighter Publishing. Come to the garden with the godly gardener, James, and his lovely daughter, Mary, and you will see why Elisabeth Elliot and Dr. Tedd Tripp so highly recommend this rare treasure.

Stepping Heavenward. ELIZABETH PRENTISS
Recommended by Elisabeth Elliot, Kay Arthur, and Joni Eareckson Tada, this book is for women who are seeking an intimate walk with Christ. Written in 1850, this book will reach deeply into your heart and soul with fresh spiritual insights and honest answers to questions that most women and even men would love to have settled.

Titus: A Comrade Of The Cross. F. M. KINGSLEY
In 1894 the publisher of this book gave a $1,000 reward to any person who could write a manuscript that would set a child's heart on fire for Jesus Christ. In six weeks, the demand was so great for this book that they printed 200,000 additional copies! You and your family will fall in love with the Savior as you read this masterpiece.

Jessica's First Prayer. H. STRETTON
What does a coffee maker have in common with a barefoot little girl? You will want to read this classic over and over again to your children as they gain new insights into compassion and mercy as never before.

A Peep Behind The Scenes. O. F. WALTON
Behind most lives, there are masks that hide our hurts and fears. As you read, or more likely cry, through this delicate work, you will understand why there is so much joy in the presence of angels when one repents. Once you read it, you will know why two-and-a-half-million copies were printed in the 1800's.

More Lamplighter Rare Books

Joel: A Boy of Galilee. ANNIE FELLOWS JOHNSTON
If you read *Titus: A Comrade of the Cross* and loved it, let me introduce you to Joel. This is a story about a handicapped boy who has to make a decision whether to follow the healer of Nazareth or the traditions of the day. This is a treasure you will talk about for years.

Jessica's Mother. H. STRETTON AND M. HAMBY
(sequel to Jessica's First Prayer)
Rewritten by Mark Hamby, this sequel will take you through the emotions of the greatest of all sacrifices. Embittered against God and anyone who bears the name of Christ, Jessica's mother is determined to take her daughter back regardless of the consequences. This is a story of human tragedy and divine love that will inspire families to take a second look at the real meaning of the gospel of Jesus Christ.

Christie's Old Organ. O.F. WALTON
This is a child's story for all ages. Join a little boy named Christie and an old organ grinder as they search for the path that leads to heaven. This is a dramatic story that has already led children to the saving knowledge of Jesus Christ. Be prepared to cry.

The Lamplighter. MARIA S. CUMMINS
Written in the 1800's when lamplighters lit the street lights of the village, this story will take you on a spiritual journey depicting godly character that will inspire and attract you to live your Christian life with a higher level of integrity and excellence. Mystery, suspense, and plenty of appealing examples of integrity and honor will grip the heart of anyone who reads this masterpiece.

The Inheritance. CHRISTOPH VON SCHMID
This is another classic by the author of *The Basket of Flowers*. Seeking first the Kingdom of God and His righteousness will be a theme that parents and children will see through the eyes of a faithful grandson and his blind grandfather.

The Hedge of Thorns. ANONYMOUS
Based on a true story of a brother who pushes his sister through a hedge of thorns in order to find what was on the other side. After permanently scarring his sister's face and losing both mother and father, John Carol spends most of his life caring and supporting his beloved sister. Biblical lessons of consequences to wrong decisions, restoration, accountability, and discernment are among the few character qualities that are vividly portrayed. Parents and children who read this story will not easily forget this dramatic but true story of the lessons learned by a hedge of thorns.

Mary Jones and Her Bible. ANONYMOUS
Another true story of a little girl whose strongest desire in life is to possess her very own Bible. Through hard work, determination, prayer, faith, and even a sixty mile walk, Mary Jones will do whatever it takes to obtain a copy of the Word of God. This true story will not only kindle a fire in children's hearts but give them a role model to follow that exemplifies hard work, faithfulness, and the reward of patient obedience.

The White Dove. CHRISTOPH VON SCHMID
This is another classic by the author of *The Basket of Flowers* that will once again lay a beautiful pattern of godliness for all to follow. Surrounded by knights and nobles, thieves and robbers, this story will take parent and child to the precipice of honor, nobility, sacrifice, and the meaning of true friendship. If you enjoyed *The Basket of Flowers*, you will not want to miss *The White Dove*.

Mothers of Famous Men. ARCHER WALLACE
Take a step back in time and visit with the great mothers of great men. Join Mrs. Washington, Mrs. Wesley, Mrs. Franklin, Mrs. Adams, Mrs. Lincoln, Mrs. Carnegie and many others and see what type of motherhood shaped such unusual greatness. You will enter their homes as well as their hearts, as you learn for the first time, portions of history rarely revealed. This is a book every mom, dad, and young person needs to read.

Other Recommendations

The Little Preacher. ELIZABETH PRENTISS
Outstanding book from the 1850's about a unique little boy, a praying grandmother, and a father who has an amazing change of heart. Families and Sunday School classes will love it!

The True Princess. ANGELA HUNT
This book is a classic that will teach children what makes a true princess in Jesus' eyes! Truly a treasure to be passed on to the next generation. Based on the Scriptural teachings of servanthood.

Thoughts for Young Men. J. C. RYLE
Powerful! "Young men, ye are weak, because the Word of God does not abide in you." Teens who are looking for a devotional worthy of its time will be greatly challenged.

Let Go. FRANCOIS DE LA MOHTE FÉNELON
Written in the 1600's, Francois Fénelon will lead you to Calvary each time you read this most insightful devotional. "The Great Physician who sees in us what we cannot see, knows exactly where to place the knife. He cuts swift and deep into our innermost being, exposing us for who we really are."

Shepherding A Child's Heart. DR. TEDD TRIPP

Let God's Creatures Be the Teachers. M. HAMBY

Let God's Creatures Be the Teachers. Audio, M. HAMBY

Tales of the Kingdom. MAINS

Tell Me the Promises. JONI EARECKSON

Triumphant Families. Audio, M. HAMBY

Mentoring Boys-Nurturing Girls. Audio, M. HAMBY

The Triumphant Teen. Audio, M. HAMBY

Life-Transforming Literature. Audio, M. HAMBY

The Strong-Willed Parent. Audio, M. HAMBY

Resolved Conflict and Restored Relationships. Audio, M. HAMBY

The Lamplighter Newsletter
Free and available upon request. Rich with Biblical insights on marriage, parenting, book reviews, teaching ideas, mentoring boys and nurturing girls, and a special section devoted to "Let God's Creatures Be the Teachers."

Rare Collector's Series I, which includes 5 books, is $65.00
Rare Collector's Series III, which includes 5 books, is $70.00
Rare Collector's Series III, which includes 5 books, is $62.00

Please call for prices on our other recommendations.
Prices subject to change

---

e-mail: lamplighter@agospel.com
web site: www.agospel.com

Lamplighter Publishing.

P.O. Box 777
Waverly, PA 18471

Toll free 1-888-A-GOSPEL

Making ready a people prepared for the Lord.
Luke 1:17